Everlive

Life is love Volume. 1

Abhayendu M

ISBN 978-93-5458-574-6
© Abhayendu M 2021
Published in India 2021 by Pencil

A brand of
One Point Six Technologies Pvt. Ltd.
123, Building J2, Shram Seva Premises,
Wadala Truck Terminal, Wadala (E)
Mumbai 400037, Maharashtra, INDIA
E connect@thepencilapp.com
W www.thepencilapp.com

Author biography

Abhayendu M is an author who is famous for his musical works and a genuine human being now living his
good life with his parents and brother. He is writing his first globally releasing book called "Ever live" his dream
and vision to live a life forever.

CONTENTS

Love of life.. 8

Values and morals 20

Aesthetics and freedom.......................... 39

Simple life... 64

Epigraph

Hello, Pursue love of life in every aspects of life as a higher ideal to live and create more of goodness, let life be the guiding light for all of us, love will show up after the most awaited times to shine in our lives.

Abhayendu M

Preface

Life itself is flowing in a way of how we are understanding things with physique itself as the sole beloved life matter here with us and more, for us through this life. Love is flowing here in all ways we can pick with our nature which is pure forever uncluttered, unshattered the most powerful entity. Here we are going in an elevation whatever we call it, let this body be our guiding light for higher purposes which in turn is our specialised sense of belonging. How come we can live a life without love for life? The answer is a no because of the mundanities happening around and to avoid it we are completely in solitude with ourselves by keeping a safe distance, just keep the aim to live forever, as love is the ultimate factor which keeps this human life a miraculous one.

Introduction

Living itself is pure like the most awaited happinesses of life, Living for it.

Love of life

Love of life here we live for the supreme love of life, we can live love of life itself here, death is not our terms to live

but our results in life can show us the way to more life. Living forever is a dream to live here we can focus on our multi-oriented way of life, skills of us can shine like a bright diamond for self, Life here is a supreme energy to cherish.Love is pure, isn't it? Yes love is through all means of its vivaciousness, helping all of ourself to live a powerfullife which death cannot reach, and life can be such a thrilling experience for soul and with life beauty becomes self. Self care rounding up whole life for preparing for more of the life itself. Life can be such a beautiful way of earning money through representation of self and living of self to higher self of peacefullness and joy. Contentment and solitude lies in wellbeing which can be fulfilled through everyday awakenings for pointing more towards life. Very good way of attitude and presence in life is an achievement of our hard work. Life is here to cherish each moment for more ways of love and eternal freedom, I do think soul get to its fullness to live here peacefully if we carefully watch and live this life, how great isn't it? Nothing goes futile if it properly nourished. The base of all starts from our body itself which is our origin in terms of this life, we are fulfilling ourselves and thriving for a better dream, this life is such a wonderful opportunity. Life will be a miracle wandering in purity with constant efforts, our life is in need of the nature around which is the aura we are carrying to attain pure energies for more, life's solitude lies in its distance itself with lives around, when we are aware about the distance and the relation, life is such a tremendous and miraculous experience to live. Our sole search for life satisfies us in a way of fulfilment and it can always help us to achieve goals in life, let life be showing us the paths to light to keep on working on what we love which is our beloved life itself, let life goes on forever like a stream in tranquillity. Be safe at our own self in nature is a mastery of self which can be acquired through understanding power of life by working towards more goals and which in turn shows us our beloved self needs more love and pleasures. When we make guides and different ways for our life to accomplish, its upto what's coming next, isn't it? The answer itself is, nothing but pure love for life in exploring its uncertainties and all the good fortunes it can bring bring with efforts with safety measures. Let life be a pleasing experience of love in terms of its quality of actions, I understood the impact of quality life terms when it comes to its behaviour of importance in making human cooperation and which happened gradually in my life and by in turn developed as a power in this coexisting space, whatever your love be a reality in its strength here life will continuously flowing with efforts. Keeping the life alone, is a big work, but in terms of its subtleness life is full of joy and miracles. Love of actions come from a nature of self uniqueness, and the truth of wisdom keeps life as a most powerful force to keep this life alive for more time and goodness will stay with us with consistency with constant support from our self. Efforts give guarantee for life's growth in this infinity we can seek opportunities for more, here life can sustain through various times in this nature with efforts we can find something may happen, let it be a vision to make something for now and future.

Life matter here most than anything, isn't it? It is our life which keeps us moving forward through this big space here its our genetics which came up within a long span of time and we can find luxuries of comforts here we can comfortably live with efforts. During the span of my lifetime till now i have lived many things in life including the death of my grandmother, life has been such tough sometimes, but the hope in us can make us move further towards more happiness. More life towards this nature can bring prosperity for attaining more life goals on this planet here life is one of the most attractive thing. Life of varieties can be acquired for strength and beauty, for more happiness within the safe space of self where we can all completely immersed in a physical freedom of tranquility. Love can be transformed within the boundaries of physical easeness, let it be a natural factor of pleasantness for us to exercise our freedom. Life is evolving through its all kinds of terrors and goodness, we should believe that the life should always settle in the path of constant love of life which make us capable to cherish all goodness in life forever which is my hope towards future. Miraculous things in life gave us the freedom for us to explore with our confidence to see life as a way of throbbing energy, life can be very soothing when we explore the beautiful dimensions of this life. I am very happy about how life has turned to the states of strength and wisdom, this life is pure perfection, let there be peace and new realms of freedom through knowledge which can elevate human consciousness to its hypes. Level of life was changing from my childhood i have been living with lots of friends, just taking care of self can give contentment in life, sometimes an offering make a big deal in our life. The biggest achievements in life can be acquired through constant practice, this life here giving us all kinds of goodness to keep our life nourished and be in goodness alone with hopefulness, the point of hopefulness comes when life comes to meet with uncertainties. Everyday seeking something far more than ourself is a nature of understanding how this infinity works and it can be a very new thing in our life or an old favourite, the sole purpose is to start something we thriving to achieve more in this life here things are all very simple when we understand everything in a good space, a good space can be anywhere where we feel at most comfortable. A right thing can be picked up with a right vibe around, life is very joyful when we are with our favourite people. Love is such an exciting experience in which the resolutions can be kept as something very hopeful for goodness and the relationships will evolve into its magnificence revealing the truth, life is we are living for the self which need to be satisfied through all means of pure perfection, let life be a lone journey of freedom and goodwill, life will succeed for the ones who thrive to get better everyday. Politeness with the self can keep this physical body at ease for more years of life in solitude, let us all cooperate with one mission to live a life full of love to keep this life a cherishing one forever, life is a success if i can live this life forever otherwise i will die as a sad man. There are lots of deaths happening around but love of life saying to me that "i wish an ever live for you so that love will never die for no one, if it shows some illusions though there will be a resurrection". The patterns of life has showed me long ways of goodness times, I am living for to experience the everlasting goodness times forever in this life hopefully. Things happening around has love, let the life flow to a place of happiness and alive, whatever comes and go life will find its place of peacefulness, Life is so good. Joyful life can give greater sense of belonging and seeking these good vibes are stepping stones to one's success in life. Life can achieve its ultimates through constant way of living and persistence in actions, life can be a marvellous experience if it happens motivated by goodness and self for the betterment of future. Aesthetic journey in life gives very good quality level of life which can elevate everyday life, i say music as a melancholy of beautiful sounds. Keeping a standard in life plays an important role in living, in relationships these standards of choices can keep us maintain a healthy distance and make our days even more brighter, through understanding this nature i have learned everything is precious in its favourable distances, it keeps on evolving. Life for all the love can be a wonderful thought but thinking about the perspectives of how this life moving here there are lot of things in life on how strange things which is reacting with us, I choose what gives me the best result and life is evolving to wonderful states of this magnificent journey of sacredness. In life, thinking about this conscious time, now and future is only left with me i can create what all needed which is now and yet to come. Self love is the most purest form of love in this existence, seeking care and love from all goodness will bring fortunes and prosperity in one's life. Life can be very simple when we think in terms of love, whatever we feel for, it is the ultimate time of now and future nature around still we can pickup our favourite things through life and life is a miracle to stay alive forever in this love, how simple life is when everything got open and our self is on love forever, just a laugh can bring happiness in us and we can live peacefully. Working environment became my everyday life and life is such a blessing through out everyday to work on something valuable, let goodness be our guiding light in this growing environment. Life is such an illusion in natures magical ways, it moves through all energies and visualising or making them is such a tremendous experience here in this infinity, what all yet to come let it be, being hopeful brings the solution for everything in this life, life is love. Everyday make it, as an opportunity to work towards life goals and when knowing the algorithm towards reaching, it is efforts and from right then life is much more easier, life can be such a thrilling experience when we understand life is here for us, the whole infinity waiting for the superstar in us to rise. I have to start something new all the time i think and i begin something in its future level of self and i see there is unlimited opportunities and here we are all safe and more, except mundane activities some people do. The distance can help to maintain a self prejudice and concentrate on life goals of ultimate wisdom of self and staying in contentment and vibrance is our work. Getting things completed in a way of a system is an evidence of human intelligence system's rise in uniqueness, when understanding things more closer we are able to function very easy in this world, human system is like a machine we can easily tune in. Lets bind all our elements we love in life and work along with it, life will automatically tuning to work with this powerful environment, each and every steps in sense of self dignity and power, keep in strength what has helped you and what has more helped you, what has helped you will protect you. The taste of life keeps life nourished in a way of knowledge which is the ultimate passion which life can attain within a time and more, now with efforts we are able to concentrate on what we need to do with our life, courageousness keeps life shining through all life here life is very precious which needs to keep in efforts for self contentment. Love is a miracle which gives wealth to humans in all ways, genuine love can heal self in all ways of goodness for the self which is our body, only love can heal our self.

Whenever our life feeling so sad there is a good time yet to come which is a new life like a flower blossoming with its beautiful fragrance, very subtle, calm and enjoyable. Life never shatter anything, life knows how to repair, its a natural way of safety keeping us to our creative sides and wisdom which we have known from our life, it will blossom again and again for love which is this infinty. Love can teach us so many things within matter of seconds, like a musical journey this life, so fresh and calming, music keeps us away to a beautiful place of melancholy and freedom. Life in its fullness which is created from efforts shows the true strength of our self and life will fulfil all the dreams and wishes. This life is made for love which is a pattern which shows the taste of life forever, in here we can live forever for the reason of love for the true self and this dream is my hope for this infinity. Love among our all kinds of relationships with unique lives around shows how big and magnificent this space is to build a life full of joy and enjoyment is this nature's true wisdom here we all are in capable to be in peace for life. Keeping life to the standards of our future needs is a miraculous idea to be more functional in this life, life is full of fun when we enjoy our day with hard work. Living is the solution here for being capable of carrying this physical existence to better levels of wisdom, it is possible to acquire what we need from nature, the ways are all open. Life is such a thrilling experience when we stick to life as a more happy experience rather than any other things. Things in life are pretty simple like this place is a colourful land to live, lots of beautiful things, aromatic environment all can help us to nourish our life to a level of peacefulness and freedom, just take few deep breaths and enjoy the calmness we feel within our physique, life here is a bliss. Mother Earth has showed us its majestic views and energy to live here peaceful, life is a flowing river which guides us to its shores of wisdom, the tranquillity of water is a spiritual energetic space which is pure like our very own existential physique which needs care and love, let all the things happen around, life is subtle for its happiness we work, let us enjoy the freedom and happiness this life is intended to. Let's have a wide view of life in terms of its quality which can blend on our physique, while considering the aesthetics and all the other aspects just like we purchase some clothes. Just looking at a thing in a certain angle changes the whole perspective, like that life can be won through very easy steps by following our passion. Life can be a wonder when we try varieties of things in life, things we love here we need to make something beautiful for happiness which will produce our solitude and in turns become our passion and work and more. Love for self keeps our life consistent through all things of life here, will for a life will lead to success, our work is solely reflect on our physique's wellbeing which keeps our quality of goodness, keeping life sacred will give better outcomes and treasures in life. Life is such a treasure to cherish every moment to its fullest. When we look back we can see how life has evolved to a form now, what is needed has to happen, life is like a creative space here we can see and sculpt our life and the base of all is we are here for the love of life, life will keep you at its best when we treasure life and we can earn more. Here our existence is based on our consciousness and future which is now and here for future too which is the now and future we can completely immerse into the magic of this beautiful creation, happiness is our choice to remain in this life to live forever if we will and it may become a reality. Love can transform life in all ways of peacefulness and freedom when we know what to use and what not, life is such a blessing to live in safety and understand how to properly, live by using things with higher potential for our growth, life is going in this high way of elevation here we are accumulating and for accumulating good we can have a choice of good with a conscience for attaining good which is what we needed for the future, and this body will react in a certain pace according to the nature of make of the things, and for us sometimes fast and slow too and it varies. Love of life is going across life consistently in a pace we can traverse towards more good, when we live this pace we can recognise the world as an energy infinite, treasuring all these energies in turn showing us what our leads is all good in terms of its life matter, what we can do is consistently work towards our dreams, yes dreams are alive, dreams can happen with strong willpower towards our goals which is in turn shows up in body as our strength, which is this existence and i wish all more life towards infinity. Life is very amusing when we can deal with life with a hopeful and contented manner. Politeness is the key to aligning to good people, its a natural factor of work towards more love which connects relations with our hard work on life can reach more levels of pleasantness. Our energy carries a certain vibrations which soothes our life with all blessings. Life energies can be kept through empathy in a safe space here everything will work for the goodness of our self and our needs. Life is sometimes taking care of others too, which reflects goodness to our self which is this only physical existential reality connected to everything which we encountering in this world at times by leaving ourself from the situation to a more safer place, with consistent focus we can develop more safer situations. Life is getting better everyday for the goodness of self and love is the answer here for a more peaceful world. Life can be a pure flow when we get enough breath, lot of body movements helps in creating a good air flow in the body, this now and next is only with us, everything else will vanish with constant hard work in life again in consciousness and future, life is a miracle for us to cherish every moment's beauty forever. Now this world is going through lots of dangers for life, Being in a position to take care of this self-centered peacefulness in actions, and add more goodness to life for wellbeing. Make focus in life in this infinity to its vivacious and multi facetedness, the journey is pure when we understand the deeper meanings of this self is to keep self contented and nourished through all good means possible which can give our self a pleasant and futuristic experience. Future is possible with our actions to keep energies for self with proper understanding and sensitivity, this sensitivity is developed through times and it can show us wonders. Alive beings in this existence share common ways to reach higher states of consciousness and future here this infinity is unique in each ways of love here, now and next what is happening keeps life contented whatever it may include futures. Possible outcomes of this existence which includes this infinite space tends to give us all kinds of experiences with our moving control towards its wellbeing, sorrows and pain, love and desire, all kinds of emotions, just like we make here to live this existence in happiness and peace. Infinite kinds of peaceful activities has happened in this existence which is happening again which is a cultivation for us to create something which can enhance our perception and infinity, in more ways of beauty and the ways of self love and in turn creates something very powerful for our consciousness to rise and shine in this space here love and infinity when we look apart and same love and infinity gives a powerful aura which is its own quality of uniqueness which is this, oneness of multi faceted life with favourite choices of our self matters here the most. Love is a possibility to transformation of infinity which can be in a state of completely engaged in life, life is a magic and "its ways of magnitudes and joy". Elevation in joy and ecstatic feelings are to be kept sacred for our beloved self and this whole cosmos have good energies to play and enjoy for our need. Whenever there is a need arise to acquire something we wish the solution is life itself, our self is more sacred than we know, we are filled with lot of love and happiness to enjoy forever, our mission is to live a life with an idea to grow and elevate for happiness which is omnipresent and powerful force which nourishes our life goals and shows us the true paths of freedom and its strength. Life is such a unique experience to cherish everyday with lots of beautiful moments and we have the power with us to conquer everything in this life, to acquire whatever we need and our dreams, yes dreams are alive for us to make and fulfil our life with joy and aesthetics, life will go on forever with its graciousness, infinity arises and life stays contented with values and morals of goodness with work and life has to show us its true nature soon hopefully. Hopefully creating more of happiness and wealth through ways of willingness which created from true strength of self love and freedom let this time be a happy niche for our ancestral paths and innovations to keep this life more and more ease, love with us is enough to guide us to all places in this place here self is our true wisdom and grace of the ultimate shining light of love is in our responsibility.

Values and morals

Earnings in life keeps on increasing we can see when we work and just monitor our life, the patterns in our everyday tasks are a visualisation of our future itself, when we move with a clear intent to achieve something in a persistent manner we can see its results in life and we can do a lot to work towards achieving more and more and thus we are recognising our dreams in a way of reality and living true wisdom and vigour of this identity, we are here free to live for a pleasant life when we understand the easeness of living here with all our traits opened up as an extension to our values here we can identify peaceful states and the courage of our life will evolve with work to better states of goodwill and pride, Life in a way is a treat of celebration to succeed our self to cherish deeply here we can be feeling ourselves far more achieved and ecstatic eith efforts now is the greatest possibility we could use to control our life to its fullest depths of contentment and sacredness of our self here now infinite. Let us unite to keep all the goodness with us to make a peaceful world more shining for us to live this love of life, here nature is not our strangeness, nature is and our work will produce more ways to reach a sense of comforts. World of joy here, let music and craft be our soulmates to enjoy this life and dream more to reach our every goals, we all are not same, we are all like beautiful gems, everything is unique, differences shows here a vibration like our similarities. Lines in a painting shows some life to it, goodness here adding up over times here every times love of self keeps us here in this observation we can grow forever, love won't subside for nothing when the fire is burning with us to live. This love keeps shining for all the good here love can transform anything it getting in touch with, love is a miraculous thing and the life here is a blessing. Lack of knowledge leads to dangers in life, its a responsibility to attain what we need to keep this life alive forever, love is such a wonderful effect when we feel it with our life in the ways of harmony. Its the time to reinvent what we know us as our self, we need to be conscious enough for the capabilities which can be built here with this body which includes the wholeness of what needs as every moments, life is moving in a pace of its pleasantness when we can tune in it to joyful. Aesthetics and its development in life are stages of this infinite space we can here do what is our solitude to make more beautiful life, life relies upon goodness which acquired to us from a strong foundation of work principles here we can find a lifestyle healthy and the elements of our foundation will lead us. People living here are of different attitudes towards life here we should thrive for life with an understanding of the energy collisions surrounded and the distance we need to keep, Life can be a solution when we are sticking to the truth of strong will of goodness and the existence is a stepping stone to the arenas of pleasures here life is strong moving ahead of time getting more stronger in life by the understanding, what of this consciousness as the accumulation and now this conscious space is sacred and it is leading us to the planes of future here we can move ahead which is a throbbing factor to life and decide what we can do about life coming, let it be a strong way of living for the sake of life here life is such a powerful tool to acquire contentment in all ways of our imagination, willpower and imagination created this world here we are the makers of our own destiny, when we understand the responsibility and forgive ourselves and move ahead we can find a lot of opportunities to thrive here in this nature, this nature has never destroyed, this is a great space of intelligence here our life is our own light. Power of self is the way to achieve more in this life, self is the only truth here we know this existence as three life stages which is past present and future, here life is completely aware when we understand the power of self which is our sacredness in this nature, imagination helps us to grow, the three stages which is past, present and future relies upon how we lived, how we can act now and in future, Living a life to deal with these energies for higher consciousness which creating life through living and loving our own self which is our physical body. Solitude lies with ones self itself, no matter what happens in life the truth of love will keep the shining lifes light alive, growth in life settles one to a place of understanding the self as sacred which is this physical body in an ecstatic way.

Pace of this existential reality itself goes in a way which is aligned to the selfs expression, through ways of creativity we can work with these different types of activities and tune ourself into the greater realms of life. Winning and losing is part of the game but what really matter is how we can accept our life in a way to create something wonderful and live to live a life and more, here death is not the answer, love can stay here unshattered through all sorts of collisions, our work and experiences in life will make us more strong with all our capabilities that we have right now to keep our life safe in this world here we are growing to more abilities, whether this life is showing some uncertainties, the things which i am aware keep me to more safe ways of love and what new and good is a blessing. We can carry this life to a more safer world with our wisdom and more choices of peacefulness, this life is a blessing here for us to cherish the wonders of solitude. Love of aspects in life is a matter of choice in this intelligent world, we can do what is needed and create something marvellous and understand things, an experience to more life in all new possible ways. Let this world happen the way it is, let us be in peace and rest, life can be decided with what we have here and more, so far we are all working to find some glimpses of pleasantness through a lot of lives which causing energy reactions with the distance we have with lives around and our choices will connect us with what we seek, life here can evolve to more level of physical wisdom and contentment will keep shining in our lives with what we have acquired, knowledge will keep this life in a shelter, this space of knowledge is full of infinite possibilities, "life" let it be we can have our beautiful times again and lets wish each other with an understanding of growth is happening for more ways of freedom and love. Contentment is the way of truth, we can be contented with what we have and more for what we need more life and there is always a solution for everything in life, we can achieve in life the things here for more love for the deep factors of life, here love can heal everything in a way of its senses of pure. Leading through life is a way of attaining more for self and when we are fulfilled with what we needed and cleared what we are looking for we have setted up, or needing to be get a new focus, we have already achieved a lot in this life including what we have learned, here life is a shelter for all, what we can dream more is of peacefulness happening in people and the existence growing to more realms of consciousness of freedom, let there be no repression in terms and the ways are all open, the way of love can heal all the wounds here life is no longer a pain with our efforts to liberation. Dreams are growing with us for more openness of our life, its easy to find new paths when we have already seen the light, the light is with us, its what we have seen, the love. Truth will never gets faded, truth is the ultimate force which keeps goodness here, life can take all of its paths through this existence, infinite realities of people creates variations in the nature, goodness will align to love for more of this kind, of beauty. Elevation here is possible to achieve through living this life, nothing else needed except loving self, which evolve in a way of increasing aesthetics to life here, futuristic ideas can keep life safe to uncertainties and there is more which is yet to vision, hopefully life is getting much more simpler in the way its getting strong. We can hopefully attain what we love in this world with what we have right now and what we needed will be our fire which is burning for the ultimate planes of liberation, liberation here is a kind of willingness itself to explore that factor of infinity which sources us to its deep sides of belonging, nature will adapt to new life to attain what we seek, seekers who are courageous enough to understand the factors of life is made through a lot of nourishing self here values and moral principles of life shows us how this world has become such a powerful place. For self this is a playful environment we need to understand the relevance of accepting everything as it is and doing what is needed, own make is solely paced with our own self here the world is awaiting for the rise of our peacefulness. Keeping life up to date with what we seek maintains this life in acceleration, love of life is never quitted, it will silently awake to freedom for the self to settle in. Companionship and the longing to be nurtured growing with us to its best possible states here hopeful life for aesthetics and love keeps the journey fearless to attain what we know and beyond, beyond this consciousness there are treasures waiting to bubble up and life is not acquiring anything less, life is a success by itself. Elevation in life gives us happiness when we understand this grow we can focus really on how to build our next steps and we are getting very receptive to ourself to understand this world as a much more infinite space. Life can develop through circumstances which is here as a possibility in terms of consciouness to explore life to live for living itself, for centuries we have been taught many things which seems mundane when we analyse it with our conscience, we are here to love this life and explore this infinite space, we cannot leave here, love is the truth and this life will keep glowing its fire with the wisdom to live forever. Learned mastery is movements when we can live this life contented here life can be most sacred and lots of opinions we can have about life still our findings will give solitude we can rely upon completely. A perfect life didn't happen all of a sudden, and it has happened too in the sense of our possibilities, we are thriving everyday to achieve more of life's matters we needed the most, with proper wisdom we can align to life in a way to accomplish certain things and live joyfully, its life which keeps us moving for the contentment here we have achieving what we needed as a life to its fullest infinities because here we need to grow this physique to its next levels we are finding solutions and our life really matters when our solitude lies in acquiring what gives us contentment, responsibility to these energies are completely falling upon us for the need of the right and true and peaceful and optimum choice we need to make here to reach our best possible stages, life is such a journey here life can happen all of a sudden to any kinds of effects sometimes and with proper plan we can achieve a great deal, just what we needed will reach us when we are passionate about life, every second we know there is this good time which no one can take away from us, the spirits in us will continue to show us its help for the infinite goodness relies here in this evolution. Its a dream to keep this good spirits with us through all the hardships here i know i will reach my goodness through whatever circumstances, I am here to live my life to its fullest, this is the attitude we all have to have on life and we are here for a life which is the most precious thing, life can achieve what we believe to its fullest extents, there is no limits in our journey, here life is our solitude and self mastery is our wisdom, love of self will keep this life alive here, love will happen again and again for the self, can go through unknown things which makes this life very innovative and giving us clarity about this existence, life here happening every seconds for the well being of our own self, when we most conscious and aware about this fact we are getting a pace of our life to live its on a fullest, goodness here will shine soon, hopefully we can have all the happiness we have dreamed, it's a opting for us to see life as a very easy thing to master and get it to our ways to make it shine bright to see our path clearly, wise beings we are, love can transform everything we have never imagined, nobody gets disappointed in this life with constant work, i know life is a constant evolution, sacredness are alive for the optimistic evolution, it shows us its presence in every aspect and every position.

Light of life is the solutions we have here as opportunities made it to sustain life in ways of happiness and peacefulness later on the paths are all clear and welcoming what is possible making life much simpler than before with the power we have to live. Life in its fullest possibilities here can be explored in a way of happiness to attain our life missions which shows us the capabilities of self as a powerful instrument to develop our existence here how we can make things more good, lights are showing the way here where we reach we can create and live, we are finding more ways to settle, life is a restful state here our physique is getting more energetic with our constant observation. Life here in constant vibrations which we will be able to find at a certain times in life here life is to live to attain our happiness which is what we call nirvana or our solitude in life itself, contented feel which gives out of peaceful activities in life which is created through lot of hardships in life here what we are seeking is continuously giving us more opportunities to understand the knowledge which is settled within us which is our physique itself, now there is of search, consciousness here we are feeling what is here, life is here attained more that we are knowing, we are moving in a state of deep rest and the connections of this infinity is this fullest perfection which i or our body. Let life shows us the wisdom to all the paths we are seeking in this world, dreams are happiness and life, it has always been in this nature, we are all loving, let the love self love. Transitions in life keeps our life very special to cherish our existence, here life happen with a force, life can make things much simpler when we derive ourselves to next planes of happiness. Life here created through constant work in this evolution here we can see everything in life as a stepping stone to our success, life accumulated over now strengthens this travel to infinite spaces of greatness here we can achieve a peace with ourselves when we are tuned with what we have connected, with love, happens again in this freedom life is very explorable to cherish and make things happen is become our routine to explore this world in all new ways of opportunities, activities in leading our life we never forget the paths of love we have treasured through out this journey in its updations too, now it is at most high, what we need it next to make it more high. Multi functional body keeps this new ways of willingness contented, what we need is here now, the power of self is the act which happens now, what we can foresee our future and living it a new dimension of wisdom makes it wonderful and take us to deep states of restfulness and happiness. Life is not a burden to carry and its a weight we got too, it is a new way we can live, initiate something every time to make things much more clear to self, what achieved here gives us the freedom to explore this conciousness as much as what is yet to come, there is no factors to fear, what we wish will reach us when it is earned.

Consistency can keep this life much more efficient when we can arrive at points of wellness and safety, life getting more safe and our innovations are building blocks to making what we needing, and our dreams are this infinity, living is our solitude, makes strength more vital for everything we need. Cultivating what needed nourishes our wealth and what happens in life won't be a problem with us anymore. We have already learned what we needing to live, its a single idea that changes our life and what needing will happen for the best with best efforts. Life is such a happiness here we explore this powerful space to value our lessons and our body is the key to what we can do further, like the times we have passed its a beautiful space and questions can elevate us to much more simplicity, life is very easy when we finding some easy ways to live this life helps us to live what our goodness is showing, what we are feeling, let it be for a while and sometimes let it go and move ourself, its a chance to live once forever. Aligned to this existential reality, let happiness be our mission, this life is much more willing than we can ever feel, let it be a strong journey to earn what we have wished, times of love and peace, restful this nature is when we can dream more, there is more ways to live, let the willingness to make something is conscious to make it a new. Thankful to eternity we can feel the happiness of everything around like more days of wishful findings makes lot more ease, this form of love takes its scales to happen more and more. Hopeful this way i know what i have seen and known, what all we are knowing, we have never accepted what we don't liked, isn't it? We know its a same path of life, unique, I and you, what we have know in love makes it more and shows how this I can know more love, this space is pure infinity and what we wish we can achieve it. Let this uniqueness with self blend in everything and life is a wisdom to fine. Aesthetics creates what we are achieving to a state of personality here light of love is life, death is no longer a lock. A love has showed what to need, so this love is never ending, it has to keep on guiding, now this is consciousness we can be free souls to attain what is our truth, movements is the solution here life is very subtle, safe paths shows us how gracious our environment is, thanking everything makes life more ways to ultimate consciousness of belonging. Life here dedicated to all good deeds don't need any worries, we are free to make our love happen in its all uncertainties and remember to be safe, likewise we can explore all the dimensions of this entirety of life. I have been wandering through my favourite time, now i can see things more clearly than ever before, this is a feel of our success we have attained. Life through all pains we can manage ourself into different things we can have choice for letting ourselves immersed in the beauty of this magical essence called eternity. Let flavours of our willingness creates what's more beautiful and the time shows wonders in capabilities we are here to lead most peaceful and subtlest life, Life is very sensitive when we give attention to every little detail in life, everything comes with a price, knowledge is the solution, I know life began a time back where i can only visualise, let the time be our friend, this physique is free from everything in this infinite space here this contentment gives us proper nourishment to more wealth which is our little secret to vanish all pains in life. What a morning, i wish everyday be like this wonderful, free, charming, colourful, creating what makes us loveable gives love and prosper will be a result of all our initiations when we care our self more than anything in this world. Time is perfect, we are done with time a lot back and we are cherishing it too here i can know consciousness and more in this world, let life is as free as now forever like all our engagements, what we desire is us for the beauty this life keeps glow. Sharing what we know now can be capable of keeping aesthetics to our wholeness, sincere willingness to make things happen for our body, sustains everything around, in its beauty and peace. Let likes and needs through what we know has grow to correct places we can feel us touching ourselves in kindness, we need some love, and its never a bad luck, its the fire within us keeps to move, I know we all are good, and we are no less or no more. We are all same people travelling in our own journeys, let everyone finds its paths to selfs elevations here life is our blessings, what keeps us alive is our love which keeps us for more, uniqueness will heal what we know and more, what we reach and we can reach more.

Let this life be a responsibility for us to make more beautiful things in life, here life can have more meaning over time when we we move further, life is attaining what we have dreamed once, its all for the good, life can sustain and cherish here with all the goodness around here life is a magical journey towards what we call it as infinity or eternity, the nature here is such that we have acquired what we know, known and what yet to happen, here life is not a troublesome place when we keep ourselves safe, life is getting better as we consciously understanding the nature as an elevation ground is, what once showed us dark now is the light, darkness is fading in our life for more light to come and vice versa with our needs, life here is building what our hard work is focused to, we are working with a life which can contain a huge amount of pleasantness here we can stay as we like with proper nourishment, what we have seen as goodness is our light, don't get ashamed for what we are, we are the ultimate factor here to grow what we are dreaming, there is no hurry to anything in our life, life is very self paced and the goodness will shower upon us for what we are as an individual life, here life is unique, what we knowing can happen for the best in this life here what we can acquire is what we believe, once it is done life will elevate to next new ways of love, life here can easily adapt to what we are living now and to next. Consciousness guides us with our good efforts to whatever we call it as good and what we seek, it is a nature of willingness we are making to arrive at a situation and travelling through these wanders are surely worth while.

Wealth can be a guide to what we are seeking, here we are facing a lot of challenges in life, here what needed to be addressed is the importance of self love and peacefulness. Uniqueness of this space we are living we can identify ourselves in most intimate way that we created this, love here sustains forever when we understand this life as a tool of transformation for what we acquired and in the consciousness to move forward to what we like, this love which happened with us which says us about conscious space and here our life is happening and for the future we can attain what we needed. Likewise a machine is working this whole infinity is running like an automated magnet, we can cater to self and move according to our love we are experiencing life, what is needed has to happen and we are forwarding this eternity to its ultimates, life is simple as it is, what we know is completely a matter of this consciousness, now its the time of self to act what is required and what else we need to focus, life is what is here is a preparation too for what is going to happen, now we have reached an intelligence level here we can live a contented life with what we have and create what we needed in ease. Events that we have faced in this existence shows how mundane certain acts are when we can traverse through and being safe in this position and the acts on developing this space to our concepts we can feel the closeness of our peaceful nature away from everything else except our love. Visions which we have created through times we have been moving, a certain time we cannot need to attain anything but what we acquired, this body is pure sacred and its our responsibility to keep this body well nourished with all good vibrations we need, Future is ahead, its a big work creating what is needed and being thankful is a way of our action which determines how we are moving, breathe and breathe, the love of freedom is with us in our body to cherish, for a moment we can close our eyes and enjoy the beauty of life, life is amazing and needed our attention at most. History has been a possibility to us never been a hindrance in the sense for making something valuable, we have arrived this much with intelligence to understand more. Like a leaf falling, time is moving with us to more goodness here we all like to stay as a lovely circle which is my hope, we are all parted with narrow lines of our own choices, and we can understand this life as a journey of lone self to its magical belongings. When i was young i never really imagined life is supposed to carry this humongous amount of knowledge, which is a possibility. There is really no worries when we are able to take charge of our self in life. Let everyday be a working solution for our life, let it be anything we have a message out of it, accept the good and leave the bad. Life keeps on carry our precious nature to all kinds of luxuries when we work, an idea in life our self gets its result with constant consistency in actions which we are calling it from ancient times as self mastery. Love is the ultimate solution that we are all seeking, wherever in life we can understand our goodness will never go in vein this way its a life we are are creating to avoid all the bad situations which may occur, anytime we can understand no matter what happens love will keep us alive for the best in life and this way we can grow our talents to our ultimate passions in life, what we know keeps more than we are yet, what we will be in our hands, we are capable of moving ourselves to all the wonderful life. Still we are living what we know, what yet to happen, it's not a matter of any questions, it is inevitable for the good and it is completely in our hands to create what is here right now and more which is our ultimate possession. Lets try not to get involved in what we believe can harm our self and vice versa with proper support and safety, what we love should sustain when we are completely in settled with our self and it will which is my hope for future. So every time lets begin what is you and i will be here as who i am, whatever happens life is a journey of this wisdom to more love and more, its a freedom to live forever, we are all capable of it and we are love. Living every moments with an ideal to keep this life nourished with what we can do at the moment here is our responsibility towards complete solitude we can know with efforts in this conscious space, its here now, what is going to happen will be very happy moments with our work towards happiness which can elevate us in this infinity, lets deal with what is we are totally in, life has never showed anything bad to us in the sense we are dealing with goodness alone, its a miracle we are living here and its our possibility to live here completely as a happy person. Whenever our body is feeling weak its a good time to leave ourself free to its flow and sometimes rest will give us what we can achieve in this life, here i am completely surrendering myself to my body for what i need, this is a way we can love us more deep, its the oneness we are feeling with the whole eternity. Travelling through all this life is an achievement here we can call what we as completely free lives, every moment we are living , its a dream to live forever here life is our will and what it will bring is our ultimate possessions. Kindest souls in this world has lived here with great mastery, what we see is the same life which is very powerful to create what we believe. Love is our light to more freedom here love can heal everything, love is our way of living here and we can contemplate our peace in lone aesthetics here what we believe is our ultimate solitude which is what will happen. When we work aimlessly what we have faced is what we needed at the most in the sense of goodness, now in this time its a reason to make something which is nothing but money. The sources of our truth is with us which is this self and when we believe the world is ours nothing else can no longer appear. Comforts of life keeping this life joyful for us when no longer anything is an obstacle and everything is a way of opportunities with aligning to whatt we need and life is viewed in a completely innovative way, here this life can happen with us our physique is our supreme tool for all the willingness and goodness we can move on to another states of beauty and prosperity, just focusing on what we love to do as the only matter of importance and our passion can lead us to success and this life is a miracle in front of us, life can be a matter of pride and wealth here when we understand the nature of all the lives around its very easy to make something happen and working for us. Lack of knowledge creates mundanity in this world here we can understand this existence as a forward movement to betterment and elevating. Life is multifaceted and our focal points will be our strength to more wealth and life is such an amazing ride to the areas of our prosperity, what we needed to do is to focus on what is needed and life is such a mesmerising journey and moves. Life is a constant settlement of development which is growing here in the sense of our growth we have seen lot of movements across what all we seeking as good and what yet to come is completely on our hands when we can accept life as a possibility to make and receive goodness, life has never made a problem to us when we see our needs of goodness alone, what we see around is what we can use if good for our need in its importance and relevance, This is place of truth and wisdom here consciousness is our revelation and what we seeking has the power to attract what we know and the best of it comes with our innovations here in the form of our creative force. Like every needs of an individual life here life acquired what is needed through constant hard work and this realisation what we call as physique is our complete self nature of this eternity, infinite here life is just a powerful tool to acquire what we needed, and its all factors of love and passion. Joyfulness, calmness are all our vibrance and we call it as our inner nature to explore what is needed, our constant love for what we call it as freedom in life gives us a chance to live what we have acquired and what are our dreams, we have never thought or even thought about certain things in life, life has different dimensions and all these energies summed up can create a big bang and our life will show us miraculous things, when we understand life as a powerful space to acquire peacefulness and happiness life is a exploration to its beauty and hope, Hopes are alive here life will show up its light through all darkness for us to find a way to the lights of more happiness and contentment. Contented here life is a happiness for our body to attain what we call as freedom, and all these elements here binded and the solutions are arriving and its here, nowhere to go it will reveal itself after long awaited times and the magic of all innovations lies in its simplicity and the power of connection generated this simplicity with the strength of our self. Let the queries of our nature be resolved with our constant hardship in our belonging, and life is such an innate force of wisdom we have here in this physique, when we are deeply involved in what we are doing life, it can be anything to nothing, life is a energy with potential to show us what we believe as our freedom is what we know it as something good within us, what yet to happen is completely relied up on us, whatever we are going through let it be a free. Nature will give what we have sown, here what really matters is what is now and what is going to happen. Whatever it is we have the full responsibility of what is going to happen, let it be a good one with our all capabilities, life has shown miracles to us and being thankful, respectful and gracious is the way of kindness and selfs quality of development. Lot of ways this life is deeply connected with us in time, time is a factor of this world we are using it to facilitate what we needed, and what is this infinity can occur is fully upon our hardships and strength, more nourishment is a way to keep this physique alive here what we call as freedom and love will help us to attain what we seek.

Aesthetics and freedom

Life is a valuable choice we have here for the ultimate goodness we are seeking, now we can at most work for the best of our happiness here every move we make derives something very special for us to take care of this life, here we are accumulating for the benefits of wellbeing here lot of opportunities we can create to work for what we needed and what we needed we are constantly in pursuit. The nature of this life is such that we can have a complete revolution with ourselves to make a better human being everyday, life is such an amazing aura of this infinite spectrum here our knowledge base is our settlement for more. Languages here formed through various cultures in the sense of its aesthetics we can see in people and the sounds has a powerful energy on who we are as unique lives. The greater there is volume the greater the surface area it can cover, likewise how our work is transmitted in this space here what we call as freedom is what is our strengths, when we give focus to what we love it's a natural phenomena to occur what is necessary. Wealth is the prime factor which is giving us all solitudes in this world, what we seeking and everything we love can be acquired with money and wealth, knowledge is our guiding light. Life is a treasure to cherish here love is keeping us passionate towards more good. Like a tree is growing our life is our solitude when it comes to any matters, our first preference is our self here we can dream of anything and achieve it with a will, Lack of resources has lead us to lots of dangers here what we can do is to collect as much as resources and which will keep our life happy and amazing. Let everything happen in the way it is, our life can make it up to a place where we can have complete freedom on our self and here the ultimate meaning is to acquire freedom in what all we are dealing with which is everything. Kindness in us nourishes our souls with what we believe and life can change its paths towards ultimate states of willingness and wealth. If there is a possibility to achieve what we believe, its a way through wealth, Our world has created to make it happen which is to collect what we believe and cherish it for our life, Health is created from a strong foundation of resources which we made it with lot of hard work and these resources can have an impact in our life to create what we believe, creativity in us is our one ultimate solitude to develop what we needed, let it be a happy one when we understand the importance of safety with what we know. We need time here to stay for what we believe and the conscious nature is our resource for making these energies towards a bright ways. What we believe here has a great impact on our physique, when we know nothing will be a barrier in our life when we can achieve a transcendence of intimacy in this world. What we believe has the power to accumulate what more in the same sense of belonging, Here we are at our highest nature now, as far as the world concerned we have everything here to build healing for our sorrows. Tremendous opportunities here welcoming life as a whole effect of goodness in its spiritual wellness. How we can transcend this life into something more powerful which has been the questions and should be. Life is a source of all kinds of tremendous things we have acquired through out this nature here what is needed has to be done. Education and morals needed to be updated and when we understand the power of our self, we can transcend this whole life to another worlds, elevation which is our sole work in this multi dimensionality here what we are facing everyday has the power and influence for what we are creating, let it be a infinite idea to build something marvellous and beautiful. Life here is with us as solutions of this era here we need to address certain things like environment, global warming and education, how we have built this like this, this is a land of all prosperity and freedom. Peacefulness is our source of wealth here what we have accumulated should support us and it is. However what we are hearing everyday, there's lot of things we have to handle in a way of intelligence which solely aims at the level of freedom and love. Sometimes a good sleep help us to generate a source of power and calmness with us and this develop a sense of belonging to our physique, yes our nature is blessed with all kinds of varieties of goodness here what we are working should make factors of our life principles and wealth is our continuous result for all the efforts we are putting here. Everyday should become a solution for us to make something better with this life and so that we are generating a function to modify this infinity and knowledge to all kinds of happiness. Life should work for us over time when we needed, its a need of time and this consciousness we are building something precious for ourselves and the main essence of all our work is to carry out our day today functions and future functions to the fullest of love and freedom. Love and freedom became so vast that this enormous world can handle everything at ease, our borders became our possibilities and the idea of oneness in world becoming a reality through all kinds of respectful actions and now the world is excellent. Life is such an opportunity to build ourselves to ultimate possibilities of wisdom and truth here gives transparency to the right situations brings equanimity and benevolence.

Life is oneness and we are feeling connected to all the goodness that we are seeking, what i have known in this world, its a tremendous upbringing about life, we can all have a connection about how we feel about our experiences. Our whole energy or what we are is our physique itself, when we are constantly in seeking what is needed which is our prosperity and knowledge. What we have acquired here has a great importance in our life and which all are stepping stones to our success here we are living in this consciousness here we are knowing something and we have a feeling towards it. Empathy plays a major role in our development and what we know is our sole matter of this existence in movements. Life is this journey towards all ultimate goals and this life itself is a magical treasure to cherish our happiness. What is going to happen is in our hands and here we can develop what we see as a good source of life. Likewise we have built all this and we are moving to further innovations here its a milestone to our life that we can live forever, love is happened here a long back and what we love is a light for us to cherish in happiness, and we are seeking more of love and goodness, what we need is to break apart our shells of mundanity to shining wisdom and we all are in to go with efforts to the continuing arrangements of our self can make a complete life. Life here can be peaceful through lot of methods we can implement and have a wisdom, life is never a pain when we understand the need for staying alive, Its a peaceful life to have a wise sense of belonging and here what we call as goodness is our moral sense and values to achieve something greater, creativity here we all can seek in the forms of our love and passion and what keeps life beautiful is the way this life has been built and the world is a place of success here people can act for a will and gain something out of the world for living life, and these patterns of life accumulates and bring togetherness to the whole life as a new existential reality, life in a way to more peacefulness and freedom here what we create has a power of love and aesthetics to the general ideas of this human consciousness and more. Life is such a thrilling experience when we understand life is important to keep this body nourished and fulfil our sacred life. What yet to come in this life plays a major role when we deal with what we can make by mean time and what to exist in this global reality, life is such a powerful tool to explore the way we can construct what we have known and what we needed. Like a flower a blossoming everyday there will be good fragrance in our life when we work towards a better future, always remember there is a reason which is to live and cherish life here we are all in need. What our life is based on to successfully accomplish the tasks which we needed to grow more here to lead a good life. Life here has the possibilities of taking care of this physique to next levels of this infinite freedom and this life is a mesmerizing one with all achievements. Love for life which keeps us alive and to have a multifaceted viewpoint towards life in terms of acquiring wealth and freedom is worthy to generate income. Knowledge here keeps us safe with what all we have learned and what is happening and the future, this conscious space we can keep our movements tidy for leading a smooth life and this way we can achieve some greater things in life. What we needed to do in life in uncertain situations is to keep ourself more safe and make a success. Lets cherish every moment for more forward life and the movements here gives the sense of living, we need to acquire what is possible for our freedom and love here what we can achieve is infinite achievements, opportunities can lead us to more ways of successful life ahead and what really matters is to keep our health in tact and this way we can build something amazing and the quality of our life will elevate to a different and best way of freedom. Life here dealing with all sorts of happiness and activities here everyday we need to reinvent everything to attain certain goals, so this world has made by us to create a cooperation. What is needed has to be done and the way we can achieve something marvellous is by acquiring the collective efforts which can make life easy and fun. Life is a solution for people like us who are hard working everyday for the needs of self and attaining freedom, what this existence is very simple and completely our physique, we need to take care of our physique all the time, what we needed in life is to keep ourselves safe in all kinds of activities, this consciousness is our sole time being which gives us a sense of fulfilment and what we needed in the future is needed to be done. Everyday what is our activities is based upon what is needed and to facilitate all the efforts we are using certain things in life, so in order for the complete revolution of this process we need to be very attentive towards all kinds of miseries and pains happening hopefully everything will be aligned to love and more sorts of wealth. Luxury and willingness to make a living for the needs of our physique challenges us with everyday and hopefully all challenges will fade away to attain a sense of wholeness in our love, here nothing else than our self exist, from what i know we need to make a change in our self in order to work with the whole infinity and there is what it is true as this life seeks what it can attain and our hardships will be a successful one with what we are creating and we have done it. This life is more peaceful than we are knowing or we know is the idea of searching for our wellbeing in some situations and life can be a success with our continuous efforts and our goals gives us freedom to attain more results from this infinite space we are living. Happiness is a true sense of belonging we have acquired here and what we need in every situation we can attain what is the choice which makes us more happy and life here is a divine experience to cherish what we love and working towards a more passionate life and this life will be greater in the sense of this reality in actions and this pieces of life arranged around will be a sense of this belonging to work with what we need and what we made here this time is conscious and more let us take deep breath and relieve ourselves for all the happiness. Lets take a deep dive into consciousness and dreams are capable of carrying us to our goals here hardwork returns as best results, what we acquired has a strength and power which our physique and what we knowing is unlimited, the possibilities arising out of all lives can be marvellous in the coming eras. What is reality what is an illusion? Its question which we can understand there is nothing, just life. What is love? What we are living right now, this consciousness and what we can achieve, imagine what all we are doing getting recorded, its a possibility to work on our everyday towards something better, let it be a creative activity and what is needed has to be done, what ever comes up in our life as a barrier we can rest for a while and there is nothing we need to do, life is such a creative space to develop what we like and what we can achieve here is a question of this consciousness and the results will give us what we needed like money and contentment, when we are able understand life as movements its easy for us to live here in peacefulness. What ever the work is when we are able to dedicate our physique to its fullest now we can see how life is changing to its superior goals of self, life is this reality we need as a good source for our wellness and creativity, like a flower blossoming let this life be natural. Life is very spontaneous in terms of its nature and what is happening here is pure consciousness, what is needed for future needed to be made with what we got and things will pretty much end up in good. Let silence be our source of goodness and life will show its graciousness when we work towards what is needed and life has all these varieties of things to do in terms of its quality and content. Life here is marvellous to acquire our initimacy, kindness is what we are seeking to acquire what we needed the most in life, the most kindest beings are us to be more and more kind to our own self. What our intent is set to be is came out of our needs and what we need is what we are seeking continuously in this infinity, here what we can make is everything and our needs will get fulfilled with our consistent efforts to elevation of this life. Mastering self is an art of conquering our self to the extents to reach to its infinite goodness and what we can easily implement in this life is very favourable to us and what is our choice makes solutions for our life, this is a vast space for all lives in this space, when we understand the power of self we are realised to attain self mastery and which is our solitude to make a good life in wellbeing, what acquired here we are living our self which is our body to keep life more and more powerful. Now what happening around we can analyse with all these inventions around and what we are dealing with is intelligence and our nature reflects our sole elevation to the infinite innovative uniqueness here we are all capable of making our dreams come alive, yes dreams are living. What we are living now is a possibility to acquire what we are looking for, here our goals are uniquely identifiable with our life and what we need is our life to ge to much more goodness. And i have this ever live dream and its my hope for humanity. Now what is conscious is now and we can align to good now for good, and next we can hopefully make it a good. We can understand right now everything is possible, its our choices of relevance automatically it will evolve to goodness to achieve what we are seeking, the nature is such that what is here right now is our choice of willingness to deal with and it will happen as an elevation with continuous efforts. The working of this existence is entirely unique for, containing shapes to acquire desired results and what we can achieve from all this is to create that we need for now and forever, this infinity will keep this love alive and what we have is the greatest possibility to achieve what is needed and more. What we can achieve within this unlimited space which is our physique has a big influence on how this cosmic is creating, now this eternity is growing to more movements here what is happening getting updated, what we know here is not limited to anything which exist and what we can love about what is our will. Right now our physique is on complete rest and what we know, something very pleasant happening to us, this experience is a good sign of growth and what we can achieve is to cherish life as a solitude of our body.

What a life this is, how wonderful people are around making life more wise with their new choices, innovations happening for all the good here what we can carry with us is our treasures and what we know has a great idea of our physique and this work is never ending, we are here completely immersed in life to live its highest areas of what we call as self, With a love for what we doing we can conquer this world, Creating has identified as a sole process of this life to make things possible and cherish its outcomes to the fullest. Infinite amounts of lives is located in this vast existence here just working for liberation is will for more and thus we can uplift our creativity to newer dimensions of this highly constructive areas. What we can achieve in this space is our possibility towards liberation here what we know is our intimacy towards infinity and we need welcoming good vibrations with our sensitivity towards this life. What we know in this life is this body we have built over a period of time and what we can do with this is unlimited here, now we can bring up self and living is our sole responsibility towards this infinite existence, here we can traverse multiple things in this life through rigorous working towards what we need. Our life is a serene nature which is our necessity to build across various outputs in life, life is such an enthralling magical experience when we needing it as the most and welcoming what we knowing and working with a culture of strong foundation structured to our life which is this complete self called our body itself. Languages have created in this world from various regions on this planet and we can see a lot of different cultures around and picking up all these accumulations in the sense of our genuineness as a being or our nature in this infinite space is an addition. When we all understanding the language of our life we can easily connect and share our life with people we like with reflecting our creative side and this way life is a best opportunity when we know the ultimate truth of this self love is what is needed. Ethnicities of people from around this globe is showing us the way people are originally mapped their movements and this space here we can do a lot of things with our capabilities, what we are seeing around everyday through various means like media etc we are coming across different inventions which are all part of this existence and when we share a sense of belonging we can really feel the nature as it is. Its an innovative place existing what we needed and how we connect with ourself in more ways of deep feelings, infinity is too what we are seeking here what we can feel around has a power of life to it, a sense of feeling arises overtimes when we are dealing with this life and what is needed is the right choices we are making and what is best is our choice to live with never giving up. Life is a creation which we have experienced a long ago in this infinity, here life was a energy spectrum in an evolving form, here what we call as life is a magical experience to open up to all new life and today our greatest innovations are all based upon enhancing our experience, what is possible here is how we are developing this consciousness and the work happening here is evolving to a level of contentment, in today's life the importance of contentment is very much significant, when we understand our life as a whole experience to cherish what we believe and what we can do with life, our life is musical and creating something relevant is an important factor to our consciousness, here we are living for the purpose of enjoying this life forever which sums up our life always seeks to live more and the world is a beautiful place to open up to new dimensions of life. In world there are lot of mundanities happening and our work will reflect how we can act upon this world. The relevance of arts in this world is ultimate and what we can create in music, media, life etc creates us a foundation to live this evolution in peace with our movements. After I started releasing my music world-wide my life got changed to position of settlement and now i can have an assurance of the life of myself can change the world of others too. What we needed to do is to chase our passion and do what we are loving to do, in sense of making money we can achieve a good position and traverse our whole efforts to newer levels of freedom and love. Love can be an amazing effort from us to make this life more significant in terms of its quality and wealth. We can accept the evolution process here and what is good happening which is a way of peacefulness which we can relate with global wellbeing and intelligence. We are all free people, when we understand what we can do with this life towards more good and developing a sense of belonging with our movements in what we are doing helps us to create an easeness and life will reveal its magical sides. Our work in life is keeping this infinity for more good and this world is a safe space for us to live this life a sacred one with necessary safety, here we can all live in peace with working towards a hopeful life and this world has provided by us our uniqueness and with all kinds of our actions to make life a successful reality for us. What here we are acquiring is only what we needed when we have a choice and we can have a choice of goodness, its a simple idea of evolution and this life is a marvellous space to create what we believe and what we can make out of our actions is how our evolution is running. Its a successful state of wellbeing which gives us pleasant experiences to what is needed and to what is happening. What we needed was all the time our beloved self resting here in all sorts of enjoyment and this life is working for all the goodness when our sole aim transit the fuel which makes fire and burns like a shining light to all our needs. Here what is truth and what all the belief system says, what we have found is our answer isn't it? It is our success to stay as an answer to ourself with understanding the goodness has never faded away, the goodness is for us. We can create something out of nothing which is the sense of belonging we have here in this environment and what we needed is to attain what is really working for us. Whatever the life has shown in terms of its simple features and elegance, life is such a magnitude to chase and observe our life as a simple way of living. Life is very good when we understand life as a complete settlement for the life to lead certain function to make this time and what we are doing in this consciousness is the relation of what we are. We go to find this element of truth and what is our choices and helpful ways we have acquired and ready to make something very beautiful and this life is a solution to our creative needs of freedom and life can throb in all sorts of joy and just have the closest movements safely with us to create a magical reality for our belonging and this sense will purify our aesthetics to build something great and what is acquiring has the possibility of creating what is needed and to create among the best possible life. I have lot friends and my idea of friendship was my life towards creating something and the life is showing me its nature of elevation with my work and the life got simplified in terms of its increase in wealth accumulated and i am becoming more aware of my self to attain what i needing, here we can understand life as a process of making what we need in terms of its simplicity and the result is our success with regular efforts.

Hello world, this was my first computer program and in this creation myself has showed me with blessings to my life on this planet uniquely and love as the ultimate factor i can keep this worlds outputs of self with me as a friendship to myself, what we can create has a great influence in our life creating what we are in belief, what is needed is a question of times and what we working on in our life is the constant action we are making from the very beginning of our life. Here we are inherited from a lot and what we can do to live this life is to understand what our deals are of ultimate seeking of our deep self, what should happen every time for the process of our life is controlled by our self, when we can arrive to a safe place its a movable feeling of existence to attain what we need as a human being. Since life has been very gracious the active parts of our lives are filled with who we are as individuals, lets say we are going to have very intimate relationships with ourselves, now we can have a friendly belonging to create what is needed and what we believe can help us to sustain what is needed in this conscience. We can carry everything to reach up through all the barriers we are knowing and the reality is there is things to acquire, life is with us in its magic which is we acquired and next, we can move and create what our relationship is creating, what is needed in our consciousness we need to creating right now, we needed to focus to make what we believe and our solitude lies in our relationship with our body. Nothingness here we are facing what we are and life is very much out of what we know ourselves. Here life is a journey to more goodness which can be said as luxurious in terms of its quality, contentment and personal standards. Our uniqueness here plays an important role in creating what we believe to reach our people to make life sustain in this time out of this consciousness and the future too is what we needed. Space is our natural surrounding which gives the freedom for us to move and live here in this peaceful world and what we can achieve about life is in matters or fractions of energy which can be concluded as our physical aura and capable of traversing through to reach what we need now or later. Like everything around this existence what all things we can achieve is a matter of our work, when we understand the needs of ourselves we can clearly focus on what we needed as individual who can support this environment in a way we have built this to create what we needed such as peacefulness and freedom. Here what we are doing to acquire the basic characteristics we have to make what we needed and what to acquire for keeping this life safe from all disasters and in order to achieve this we need to collect certain knowledge from everyday which reflects on our life, here what we believe should be what we love and the freedom and peacefulness helps us to keep our body very calm and composed. What we call as more freedom and beauty in life is our needs to welcome more goodness. Here what we can achieve about life is the living itself and more, we need to work hard in order to get what we need and what we can achieve through a life full of happiness is purest forms of this self. Most of the time happiness is our choice when we are the only one with us through all the times of hardships in this life now what is relevant is how we can procure the needs for a better life. So here love is a transformation to access our own innate characteristics of selected goodness and what we call as mind is the same selected goodness in powerful nature. Life is a powerful force and when we are able to concentrate what reality we need in this infinite space, we are making a pact with ourselves to create a better human being in this consciousness and what we can do about making it happen is through understanding ourselves in the way of revolutionising and recognising individuality. How successful people like us we have created this world from what we know is how we are doing to acquire what is needed to work with us, on side what it can deliver to us to keep this happiness fulfilled for what yet to begin, our creative space is the most expressive space for us to initiate what we believe and is to achieve a more aware and liberal freedom to express and inculcate what is our life in this existential reality. Reality is what we are creating when we need access to what here is known as our intrinsic and needed capabilities, what we can do with our physique is to develop capabilities to align to our needs in terms of life's quality and needs to create something. What is good and what is bad is our knowledge of consciousness for future too, what we need is our movements and next steps in life, what we know in our life is our treasures and what we are going to live an elevation came through goodness with our hardwork and dedication towards what we needing. Life as a source of goodness we can transform our self to ultimate elevation when we considering life as a one journey here we can make what is good with our self with continuous revolution of our physical self which includes what we love in this infinite existence. Life acquired through all means is what we can derive out to inform and avail greater spaces of living. What is our truth stays as our beneficiary around this world for living this existence in uniqueness to infinites and more. What all things we are gathering and whatever ways of lives are living around, here coping up with self and this multifaceted aura reality is our freedom to create success. Successful career choices can be made through rigorous ways of developing our skills and making more efforts to create beautiful ways of living standards. Here life can be magnificent with what we are developing and what is needed to acquire for more ways of practical knowledge and to understanding the theories as a foundation for our self structural development. Spiritual processes have been a part our life and now it has evolved to another levels of innovation which creates subtle ways for us to live peacefully and these ways of goodness creates what we believe to achieve more of personal freedom. Here what we believe is the factors of life and its achievements in a way to acquire wealth for what it is standing for which is nothing else but our nature of goodness, its a dream to create this physical body to a bigger picture which can make the effect of pleasantness in solitude in all the times and by providing infinity what we believe through what we know as the results. Eminent and the qualities and features which can relate with our ultimates here is a blessing. Here what we need to believe is a gratitude to our self which we are knowing from very own existence, what is needed is the right living for more of good and this elevation can give what it really need focusing to make new creations in the truest meanings of love, freedom and needs in this eternity. We can achieve a proper way of living, an ideal of our self-love with an attitude towards life to create something marvellous, what human perception always seeking is to create something more special than what we know and here its an opportunity to work for the same in the sense of relevant to consciousness of now and future. Music, dance, drama, painting, other works of all good nature is all what we know as our supreme qualities to exist here in this world, how we can relate with these elements of goodness and to make a living out of these ways and thus we know what we are doing is good and keeping our everyday luxuries to the fullest of its highness for ourself.

What is happening today, I am wondering everyday when I wake up, life is just a matter of perception and this life is scattered around like a vast cosmos, how this infinity is created, through evolution. Now what is relevant is how to make something to give us what we need, the answer is one life itself, gathering what is needed and making it to happen for what our life should be, is our responsibility, its a big journey and when we reach our solitudes at times, we can be thankful to our self for everything. It is an easy life here with our work our life gives us our solitude and what we needing will be our questions again to solve for what we needing. Our careful life made us who we are today here what we needed is to understand where our journey belongs, it is self love here what our love for ourselves belongs to the reality of what we needing, here we got lot of possibilities, our life is very infinite in our own magical ways, keeping this life very safe to work for ourselves is an everyday task to complete what we are aiming for, let the aim be a good one, truthful to our dignity, whatever we do we have the truth one our side to make this life to the best openings. Life is a tremendous opportunity to live and to make life happy and beautiful. What we needing in life is to make what life is achieving and what life is going to achieve and to see life as an opportunity to make this like attach to something very powerful force which our self, our uniqueness is our life here which keeps us more alive and what we need is what we are making out of this consciousness and plans to make in future and let our needs in future be safe and subtle with all the efforts to retain our self in happiness and safety. Life taking this way i am saying what there is a possible love we need the most, we are here to live the love and live beyond and the achievements will satisfy us and again start working for more achievements. What to believe in this infinity, its a question of deep rooted knowledge and this consciousness gives what it is, the answer is believe, believe ourself, how to attain what we need, here? Here I am the supreme authority of my wellbeing, whatever happens in life through out this life our self which includes our likes is our only wisdom which giving us what it is needed. Lets say about movements, Movements, its a culture we are generating for our self so whatever beliefs we are chained we needed to understand this freedom of our self chained will exist in uniqueness. What all things everyday this infinity is containing, what we are is just life to be capable of solving what it is we are making for us, ecstatic ways is our legacy here to live in peace, whatever we are knowing its a blessing in the name of love. Self is our love and what we make is what our needs needing and by creating our self creates next steps to elevation and this existence is just renewing with our work, and there is lot of other things too which is creating in more outside ways in this eternity. When we live this conscious which is all the times "the now-time" what we can make up to create what we are capable of, and what is our generations, we need to face our intelligence to keep our self safe, and what is the light we are in need, we need to do an assessment for the betterment of self. Let this journey of our solitude connected and leads tasks by ourself to completion, lets unravel the mystical sides of this infinity and happiness we can be making as our true wisdom. Likely to every other incidents in this world our self and our likes needs to be placed in a position of this love and care, here what we know never fail us, its a victory to attain. In addition, high concentration of life energies has a story to tell of this identity, let it unravel by our work forever. I am with love, this is the mantra we are generating when we are seeking goodness continuously, the money will flow to us with hard work. Money is the form of life we are in tuned in this energy space here what we needed will happen with our movements. What here now we are making our self to its new levels of greatness, everyday we are waking up and its feel like a new day, and this life is blessed with so many things and living itself is a gracious power. Power of our identity is reflected in this infinite space as a vast explorable goodness and what we can arrive every time is the best of ourselves. What is our need everyday is to collect some money or plan and work to make some money to make our life safe, so what this life can achieve is our goodness to elaborate in this infinite cosmic to bring what is our next possibilities. Here what our lights has achieved been with us here from the very beginning of our life, and what we are in need now is to accumulate money from what we do to make the best possibilities, now what we can achieve here in this world with our creative wisdom is unlimited, now what is our future is? It is solely depending upon what we do and what else we can accomplish. Consciousness here in terms of our movements gives us wisdom to live this pure life here what we needed to make in this conscious time is our legitimate factors of wisdom. We need what is possible and our truth will lead us to what yet to know, with all our good intents, what we can achieve here is our best life, and what is our futuristic concerns which will elevate our consciousness to make what is best. Attaining what is needed is a way of power of plans and making the outcomes of this infinite consciousness a success is what is needed to create a successful life. Life here at times is a way of observing our wellness in tied up with the sequential money generating terms and here what we can do is a lot. A sovereign authority in our life should be most legally our self in a position of our legal status comprising the permissions we have, here what we can achieve with this authority is keeping life safe and secured in this infinite existence. Contented love we are feeling and the graciousness we are feeling towards everything here matters in terms for our quality of life and generations of aesthetic capability filled good quantity of life matter which can be self related to creative expressions in movements. Offerings towards what it is created for work to generate money and with love we can transform what we are in need of at most. Here spiritual life is our serenity and to make wealth we need life which is our matter to release to what a surrounding, to place its quality, in deep meditative forms. What life in terms of the space in grace, with our hardwork we made it, and now we are again seekers of our own solitudes. Just like a light is emitting our work we are capable of producing our life as a better way of communication and useful in everyday life. Like what we need we need more and more power to control this energy, we can start accumulating and for living itself we need a certain amount of knowledge to keep this life alive. Our intelligence referring to our physique has grown in an enormous way from our childhood till now and we can understand this mass can be nourished and nurtured in need to keep up with big life happening with us. Literature and through literature we can develop a sense of harmony in this nature, growing with our needs this nature is so peaceful in its senses of truth. Educating ourselves is the most common responsibility we can take in to action and this whole world is a super powerful space for us to create what is right. Peacefulness in its aesthetics built from generations of work and this world is a place to protect and live with magnificence. Unlikely to the achievements what we have the outside responses in life may vary, what we need to focus is own our goodness and with most thankful way to our own self and forgiving others and ourself for what we need to make. We are the supreme authority of our nature and its a big work to create what we are on developing. Here our setups fix our needs with in a time here what we can achieve with what we have is enormous, when we know we are not liable to anyone for our freedom so what we can do to make our life special by treating our self. When we need what we need, its a question of what we are attaining, and the results will get better with constant practice. Here what we can learn from this world is infinite and here the money can be increased, in consciousness we can derive what is happening and what we lead will elite with constant efforts. Here our time can be divided for our lifestyle and what it can bring is, what we need as a support during work and what this life is achieving, through achievements we can earn more. Our life is a varied circle when we can see this world as lot of possibilities, our fulfilment in different life matters and it keeps on multiplying as our strength and life is such a hopeful journey in terms of its goodness and we can see life as settled when we arrive at a position here we know we can achieve what we needing. Life is a strong way to make sense for our self to live this existence and while understanding the nature we can create what we need with our craftsmanship and elevate our self to multiplied energy solutions to achieve money and the combination of all this is one, one life to create what we need and the aesthetics founds in our life with constant efforts. The importance having fun at everything we do is most important, here what we need is a good times and we can make it with our constant efforts to wellbeing. What is our self is here now our self is this consciousness, and what we need in future and in making this life the way we hoping, here who we need to address is our self, and self practice will go to what we do to making our life which is our money, we can make a successful life happen with constant practice and with loving our life. Here life is what we create and with precautions we are able to support ourselves in times of need and what we are relying is completely our self. How this world is, we are living a way moving up till we feel satisfied and the love of life includes all these satisfactory elements which we can say as our strength. Our relationship with people can be evolved to such a good states of lives and with efforts in consciousness we can develop a wealthy life with a set of people and the existence is a co-supportive system to create what we dream and what is our making can be with the best output. And what relies with our strength is this evolution of uniqueness here we are in constant seeking of love and pleasures, what we need to do to contain ourself more responsible here is to keep earning money everyday. Self can be derived in a way of consciousness and future here we can monitor ourself as a leader and a true strong person of the one symbolism of love in our life, what our strengths are here we can make best out of this consciousness. With a proper lifestyle we can update the way we are right now and make use of this consciousness to its heights here what is our implementation has to be a comprehensive effort for innovations. What is our aim in life is definitely created from what we know as good and may be what we need as a good aim in our life like making legal money, here our dreams can make a uniqueness in the world to achieve more and fulfil our life goals, generally what everyday we are knowing this life as a complete way with ourself, this life is our strength to achieve more money and what ever we can imagine we can manifest our life towards our goodness we need and this connections comes to reality as our supreme results of our knowledge and life will show its strength that we are powerful, we are this physique itself. Our imaginations has our own capabilities and what we know now as a trouble becomes and evolve as tomorrows best time and don't forget to stick to goodness, in this consciousness what we are earning will gives us strength and with love this life can be focused to better outcomes with constant support from self and this life will be revolutionised in to its rebirth cycles and the life of this new human arise from nothingness to infinities. Now what we own and what we are knowing and what is our need and choice and what we love is what we need and what we are seeking is for our goodness, what we can work with in this consciousness is now what we can creatively achieve, let it be any work in our life, let us find solitude in developing ourselves consistently to reach more and more. When we are understanding life as a purpose to enjoy this life we can find happiness everywhere and our life will be in complete solitude. Every day we are waking up and what our life is, we can see life as very simple things we do with ourselves in our daily times. Everything in this cosmos can be earned with a mindset to achieve what we believe and the freedom is ours, in choosing what we are. We are what we believe here, we don't need to worry about where our thoughts are right now, we can just immerse in what we love with simply choosing.

Simple life

Magnitudes of this life we can explore with our work in life, Life here teaches us only one lesson is to simply live, so what this life is, this life is our accumulation of what we have created and the responsibility is fully ours to understand there are lot of mundane things too in the world and our life is completely in solitude for happiness and this infinity is our belovedness here what we call ourself is what our physique is. What is our moral conduct in this space keeps our friendship very closer with what we need, our self needs what we like to do and when we are aware what is our intentions on our life we can clearly move ahead to what we needing. What is our intentions and where does it came from, what our intentions is what our needs are, when we are finding more ways to creative freedom of expression and find ways to sell what we need we are creating a future of prospects. Here our journey is most welcomed to us and we need to know this is a very safe place to live with all precautions, when we are aware what is all our interactions with people we can create a life more secured and with the understanding that we are in need of our attention. What our time is devoted, this precious nature made by working has given us all altitudes to life in various patterns and what we are making out of this is our happiness and power. The power of our self lies in all kinds of goodness we need in this life and what we can achieve from our life is this life which is our ultimate passion. Life will get high here with passion and what we needed is how we can traverse to next levels of our life, what we are seeking is completely based on what we know and what we like or what we need so what should be our intention is to safely live with contentment in this world, our sound is very good to attain what we needed and what we need to focus is how we can produce quality in this environment. What is our surroundings has an innumerable power to change lives in matter of time and here what we can in sake of our own personal development. Here what is the truth, we need to involve in work for ourselves to find our truth, what gives us solitude is our truth and what is this life made up of, life is an accumulated energy source for what we are and what we are going, we are further moving to what we need and here life is such a simple act to develop a sense of belonging to our goodness in comforts we can make with consistent efforts. Right now or self exists here which is our body and what this consciousness can evolve to newer life and when we consider ourself as love for this self and this nature here is a mere reflection of our strength and life is a solitude, what is our life now, with proper analysis we will be able to get to an answer, our life is our longing for our self love and care and here what is this time can tell us is our work here will make more of that we need for more of this life. We can assure the clarity of our results as our solitude itself, solace which life brings from our moves and our beloved nature is our strength to attain more. Here what we needed to address is our life is a complete solitude and we are here to live forever. What we need this life for when we truly understand our solitudes are needed, full love we can create with the knowledge of love for this never ending life, now our life will work in terms of life powerfully, and here what we can achieve is our strength to live more. The nature we can create here in a way of goodness when we understand its deeper meanings of self and life is such a solitude to understand how this life can achieve what we are in constant need of, lets say now we are in need of money and life is structured in a way of making money happen to us with the help of all goodness and our hard work will lead to more money and life can be in such a peaceful state. What is our knowledge is, when we understand this nature, life is our physique and what we are accumulating here is our possibilities to strengthen this ways of physical strength, and peaceful ways leads us to matters of this energy spectrum and this infinity is our longing to live, here infinity is created as the most beautiful creative way in which life generates all kinds of innovative ways and everyday is our way of life, happiness is a matter of our wellness here what we can achieve along with what we are, we are in need and for more we are constantly working, and being in a state of solitude shows us its a good time here for life when we can properly arrange our life's multi oriented opportunities and earn more. Focus is what is our effort and the paths to creating an infrastructure and let it be anything in this life. Life style and willingness to change is our love for what is needed, here what all we have acquired we can traverse things in a way of understanding and this life is a powerful force to create what it is essential. Like all the love of this life what we needed here is what this infinity is when we can identify our life in what we focus, here our life pays for what it is our life, the real sense of belonging, the real affection which is all feelings to our self. What is our primary decision to make this life full of happiness, we need to make our life go forward only for love, here life will show its graciousness with the power of our self in need and what all we are going through this life, our life will reach to its love with constant efforts, and here we are free to love with proper knowledge for ourselves to keep our life safe, and we can make this space a magnificent one. Like all our days of goodness what we can achieve here is of prime importance and what is needed in this consciousness is to be made from our efforts and with constant precision we can achieve what is needed for our future. Like a painting our life is such a beautiful way of living, isn't it? Life is, when we know the truth of our wisdom leading us to where our self should be in complete solitude, this life is such an amazing ride towards all the wellness and what is needed will happen. For our own sake of this traverse in this existence what we can achieve is of prime importance and what is needed is our willingness to answer ourselves and the right choice will happen to lead. Peacefulness and freedom we have known from centuries of oppression around and there is mundanity in this world when we are aware of our self as an elevation we can traverse ourself into better love and this way we are making a unique movement which can revolutionise our physique into greatness. Love can transform this world in to what we dream of and what is needed is right here, consciousness is what is happening here now its our involvement which keeps this life sacred and our mission is to simply live, life itself is joyfulness and in future what is needed will be our responsibility to function here as we love more. What is here which we like is our complete solitude and here life is a blessing to live, and what we can create with this now, we have our vivid imaginations and what is possible is right now happens if we strive for it, whatever barriers in life occur and whatever needs in life is needed to be. Here life is our complete solution and what is needed is our sole purpose of developing this self and what is required should happen with this life here, life is a bliss. Here what we can achieve with this life is enormous and what we needed is our right choices when it is needed, according to our like the good will happen with good efforts for sure, here what our belief systems possibly is structured and in a way we can see everything as beneficial and what is needed is right now how we can act and this movements here happens for all the love we can imagine. Our imagination is our light in this world here our dreams are achievable with what we strongly believe and our intuitions are helpful in finding the truth for ourselves. Whenever a trouble occurs in our life we can find a solution in need and gracefully living in this place is our valuable asset. Whatever comes across our life this life gives us complete solitude and here we are free to earn what we are in need of with right efforts towards goodness, what is our needs in terms of this life, lot of our wishes are our journey towards more liberation and here this system is a support for us to grow towards the ultimate possibilities. Altogether what this self is capable of living here with efforts simply by earning the magic of life which we can feel here and this life is such a wonderful opportunity again. Likewise how we live in this planet we can assume a lot of things and our intuitions guides us to what we can succeed, and the success is ours. Here we are all unique beings and how we can manage what is right for us by producing the adequate amount of standardising our life to reach a point of wealth, here we can all earn what we seek by attaining goals through, efforts of infinity. Here who am i is our answer to the infinites and what we believe here is what we need and the life is such a tremendous opportunity towards a happy life ahead, and what is our future, here we have reached at points here to control this nature to an infinities of safety and here goodness will be our light, and this way what we are perceiving is ultimate. What is this infinite space here what we acquiring is our wealth and this body is our space to make what it is possible here and we are in this consciousness, the time is now to pickup what we like and the journey is never ending, here what we can achieve is more than our thoughts and imagination. Here what we built for the nature to understand this life as a true wisdom and here there are mundanities around and with efforts towards keeping a safe distance with all we can find something out of this infinity and we can avoid our past situations gracefully by understanding the life and fearlessly we can be moving towards. Meanwhile some mundanity still leave to infinities. Here we can forgive ourself and which is the quality of great nature and with proper force we can be building ourselves to a strong position and rest what we can work for the future. Here this life I am knowing a lot of types of relationships, what our ultimate nature says is our quality of living this self will elevate with knowledge and time and what we can achieve through any kind of situations are milestones in our life, here our strength is our truth and life will show its wisdom in return of our hardships. Like a day beginning, from sleep till we go again to sleep its a routine which we can make to work for what is needed for us, its the money we are creating with our goodness and this work and our earning will support us in developing what is our future depended on responsibilities to our self and our likes. Our future is safe when we are enough full of quality, its a good time to analyse what is moving forward to our next time. Here works towards a binded life we can feel this whole energy making life as a combination of goodness and happiness, these things which affect our life to an extent of how we can carry it depends on how we are moving and life is very simple when we know living is easeness by simply living. Life is extending its capabilities with our presence here what we can achieve is of what is our needs and dreams. Life has been such a marvellous journey and when we are trying something very innovative in life everyday like just waking up and we are getting a feel of this new day, we can imagine what all we needed to do today and just by simply enjoying the surrounding we can find peacefulness and solitude within ourself and we can start creating. When we try moving and to find the things which we needed to create for our love for self and needs what it is needed here life is power and we can conclude this life to a state of living forever and its a dream to live forever. What it is to pick up something which we needed everyday and the way we have arranged our life space keeps this life easy to pick up easily and our physique well and in complete wisdom we can move further to what is needed in this consciousness.

What here in this era we are making, our sole focus has transformed into a new level of life here what we acquire is what we are living. What we can achieve with this whole existence is our life which can make a unique presence in this infinity here our love makes what all terms we are getting to work with we can identify all of it as a sole path to freedom and wealth. Here finding self love is our wisdom to live this life here what we can achieve is the sole matter of life in this existence, what all these things we are facing everyday with our life we can find all these elements as our growth factor to what we need to achieve, let it be our dreams and imaginations which includes passion to creativity and knowledge, here life is our solitude and living is our wealth. Money can be achieved through various efforts here what our truth will lead us to laws and this consciousness and future is all ours. What this existence can give is a glimpse of this consciousness and what we are living this love for all that we adorn and what we need is not far, we can move hopefully, it is this infinity, It's all love. Let our needs be our sole element of work towards a better future here what is this human relations we acquire is what is we can have a choice of love. Love can be acquired with our work towards a better love. Here what we focus become our reality and don't forget to strongly keep the grip, here what we need is to access our realities of life as evident matters of happiness and what we need to achieve it through rigorous ways which can enhance us into more detailed understanding and easiness of life. Here what we can achieve is to generate how much of income we need to access all that we need and for this what we can do is to love and work towards it, here life simply living is the factor of presence which can produce our life better in every ways, life dedicated to life for a life and this life is never ending love. Here what we needed as the most delightful way of living and what makes life so simple, here only life matters to what we can earn and our happiness is our presence for keeping this everlasting love for the supreme self. Here what to do with what we call as our light of love, keep the light with us to burn till ever to create what is our at most important matter which can acquire what it is in making of this time of consciousness. Here what all things which matter to us which can produce better results in a way of our perception and finding it all in ways of understanding this evolution a true wisdom to our personal wellness and which in turn brings freedom and life. Here what is life as a real strength to achieve a human's wellbeing, what is we calling as love itself here as a reason to make what it is, the future came to a relationship to deal with what is going to happen and this way we have achieved a real standard to create a free constructive life. Standards in a way of dealing with what we call as true wisdom of our self and when we feel alone its a good time to think and take care, what we call as freedom is what is of at most importance and we need to make a movement here to achieve the deriving result to make what it is reality oriented with our life. Here life is matter of times which can formulate to create a wellbeing and this life is such a simple act to keep it safe and through recurring ways we can arrive at decisions which is kept this life as a true symbol of wisdom and life going to happen again here what is death, the term death itself means life leaving ones consciousness and here love for life is never going to happen when there is death and what this infinity tells us is life is going in ways of more love here we can bring all kinds of nourishment to keep this life alive and after a sleep what we feel now is what we can feel alive when we are tuned to perfect health and here what to feel happy about is our life's simple things and the easiness is our nature to live more. What in life we feel sudden outbursts of energies and we call it as some movements and we can develop to relate these in very similar way and these movements here can make things really happen to make love a possibility to live for what is our desire in wonderful life. Here how human intelligence is made up of when we understand the life as an opportunity to make more wealth is what is keeping this life towards matters we are in tuning with life, Here we need to like to make love for what we need and what is essential is making the perfect choice which is our long term life, here goals for us as innumerable are our self here need support and supports what we believe and what is this journey all about our hardwork to attain a perfect life. Our life is just perfect as by simply living here what to do now and the question connects with the conscious time and its relevance making us to attain a force to go ahead. Where is this life going and to where exactly we can make efforts, here life is no longer a trouble when we are growing up to each stages of life here what we believe is what we should do with proper knowledge and safety. With proper nourishment in life this physique will be capable to attain what is needed and in all activities around our life life can succeed and find solutions and contentment. Solitude in life is capable of giving us what is needed and to what extent this life can be strong here in this consciousness living is our conscience and this time which happens every time we enjoy this world as a settled source when we are capable of keeping this physique calm and strong for infinity. Calmness will occur automatically in our life and here what is our goal, is to attain what is needing, What we feel about ourself is completely our uniqueness and this self can be manifested to other sources of happiness in this elevation journey and we are capable of striving and attaining more for what it is. The solution is our intimacy towards our growing life here what is needing is what we can accumulate and the accumulation is our strength and what is this world will be with our constant effort it is also changing to reach our goodness, Here life and this existence are not separate in the sense of our growth when we understand there is a whole lot of other things too in the world we are capable of attaining a mindset to face the world to reach our infinities and what is our moral values towards certain global issues, what we can live here is our self alone so what we can be safe in this consciousness and we can decide a peaceful and lovable life for ourself, what happens in the nature is our own willingness to living.